T0165315

like smoke rising, like wind

Kathleen Galvin Grimaldi

authorHOUSE®

AuthorHouse™
1663 Liberty Drive
Bloomington, IN 47403
www.authorhouse.com
Phone: 1-800-839-8640

© 2011 by Kathleen Galvin Grimaldi. All rights reserved.

No part of this book may be reproduced, stored in a retrieval system, or transmitted by any means without the written permission of the author.

First published by AuthorHouse   05/12/2011

ISBN: 978-1-4634-0696-7 (sc)

Printed in the United States of America

Any people depicted in stock imagery provided by Thinkstock are models, and such images are being used for illustrative purposes only.

Certain stock imagery © Thinkstock.

This book is printed on acid-free paper.

Because of the dynamic nature of the Internet, any web addresses or links contained in this book may have changed since publication and may no longer be valid. The views expressed in this work are solely those of the author and do not necessarily reflect the views of the publisher, and the publisher hereby disclaims any responsibility for them.

Contents

in
memory
Of
Mom

"Peg o' my heart"

Margaret Brett Galvin
1907-2002

Prologue

like smoke rising, like wind

I remember what my mother told me:
Blood is thicker than water.
She was in her fifties, then.
Did her mortality force her to speak
of a truth she had learned through loss?

Family was everywhere, everything
when the youngest of seven.
Yet she learned Loss's truth
through a mother, when young and when leaning.

The youngest of seven and everywhere
a mother's face, a laugh, the touch
of a mother when young and when leaning,
then gone—like smoke rising, like wind.

A mother's face, a laugh, the touch.
Loss etched into the soul for safe-keeping,
then gone, like smoke rising, like wind,
surfacing oddly—only now and again

as memory, thick, coagulating.
She was in her fifties, then.
Family blood—lines were thinning.
I remember what my mother told me.

like smoke rising

"These are the days when birds come back,
A very few, a bird or two,
To take a backward look."

`Emily Dickinson

Center Stage

When memory moves
to the mind's center stage,
the house lights dim.

A hush hovers over
the vast, empty space—
waiting,
just waiting.

One by one,
the colors of my soul
rise up, shining

out of the shadows
into the spot-light

as a flickering first,
then steady flame.

This is their time,
their place . . . .

Mom: In Retrospect

I remember our three family house
with the blue spruce topping the highest porch
and my tears in the back seat of the 39 Chevy
when Pop dug it up as a tiny tree from a field
at night to bring it home. Forsythia spilled yellow
all the way down the bank at the end of the yard
in Spring. Seven sister roses played all along
the bent black wire fence in Summer. You always
wore an apron newly pressed from the line,
smelling like April showers even when it wasn't
April. Your mashed potatoes mounded every
main meal. Huge globs of butter sliding down
in rivulets while you whipped them around
and around In the pot. You baked ginger cookies
every week, soft in the center, filling the cookie
jar that sat cracked on the top of the washing machine.
Two cookies and cold milk at your kitchen table
made the world complete, compliant. That house
always smelled like "Come in , sit down, put your
hand into the cookie jar." You had me believing
that life would always be so. A picture you painted,
never to fade, even long after that jar's final
emptying.

Teddy-bears, Go-carts, and Other Lost Things

"I was only seven, and when I turned the corner, I saw them playing football. It was my teddy-bear, the closest I ever came to having my very own doll."

I look at the old woman sitting on the bed next to me. Her voice trails off as she travels down some path long lost and remembers.

"And then there was the time they took my doll carriage and made it a go-cart . . . ."

She stops.
Her eyes hold the memories carefully, caressing them in quiet intervals.

She watches the long-ago.

I remember, too.
Her eyes were once crisp, blue,
darting first one way, then another,
always charged with an inner electricity
that pushed itself onto you
while she talked.

I look at those eyes now—
hazy, grey, misting over with memories
of other faces, other times.

The electricity is gone.

Only yesterday is alive.

Her brother once told me
that when she was four
they found her sleeping
on top of her mother's grave,
a crumpled bunch of black-eyed Susans
in her hands.
She had walked two miles
to bring them there.

Maybe life brings us all
full-circle before the end.

For her, back to her mother's grave,
waiting for a comfort
that never comes.

Victory Gardens

Patches of earth with no value,
Victory Gardens they were called
on the home front in WWII.

Family, tending to its own,
waiting, watching wily plant tendrils
winding their way into bed-rock blossoming.

Even in bloom, all wasn't safe
in the back rows reserved for tomatoes,
or nightly where my father sat

cutting holes in Dixie paper cups
carefully, like a surgeon concentrating while operating.
Hands holding devouring danger at bay.

Mini-lampshades, upside-down,
signaled victory for the yellow blossoms.
He knew only cupped ones survived.

One by one, inserted over yellows,
row by row, he'd bend low
stooping, rising, "jesus christs'," ripped cups.

He tended his patch paternally,
everything worked for, nothing went wasted.
Idle hours forged into winter's food.

Canned and sauced and relished,
even greens yielded piccalilly on bread,
with juices oozing, tickling the chin.

The war wheel continued to turn
The cogs, no choice to say—
"No, not that—not ever again."

Yet fruits were pulled from dirt,
while the wheel, continuing its turn
yielded winter, when summer was spilled on to plates.

In the Dark

We never said much
sitting in the dark
on the third floor porch

watching for the next streak
of white lightning to whip wildly
through the open black spaces.

We never knew from where
the next flash would come.
Expectancy hung in the air

between us as a palpable thing:
immediate and all-embracing.

As father and daughter,
it would always be so.
Shared silences could lighten my soul

while it sat,
waiting for hope,
in the dark.

My Brother and Me

Back then, we were different.
My eyes were dark, yours blue.
Your hair, light and straight.
Mine black, with long curls.

You were quiet; I wasn't.
We were separate branches
growing each our own way
from the same solid trunk.

And you knew how to worm
your way under my skin.
You'd pace yourself always:
few words, deliberate steps.

A partition separated our rooms,
yet you knew how to grab my attention.
First one sock flung high, then another
not quite making it over, perched

on the top until coaxed loose
then down with the end
of the broom handle
when wash day arrived.

How I hated those socks
so dirty at day's end
on top of the pink roses
rising up so high on my wallpaper.

How you could insinuate yourself
into my life every time.
Masterful. Leaving your mark.
As the years passed,

and you grew into
my older younger brother,
how I learned to take
such comfort from just that.

Long Gone

I grew up in a New England place called Bunker Hill,
like the battle that won who knows what from who knows
whom.
Even the hill part was lost long ago under wavy asphalt
winding along turns toward a summit no longer visible.

Three family porched houses crowd its beginning
like onlookers at entry point for a marathon.
Only further along and up, the more open spaces.

Bicycles boundaried a world of long green lawns
bordered at each end by a drugstore with swiveled seats,
glossy counter, vanilla cokes, ice-cream cones-double-
scooped.

Penny candies lining the shelves next to the cash register
called from colored papers to be shoved into pockets
as legs touched pedals for the next lulling laps
interrupted now and then by shoe laces untying,
swings to be swung at the corner park
friends gliding in along the way.

"Don't forget, be home on time for supper!"

no fear.
no warnings.
no predators lurking along the hill
nor in a young mother's heart.

Summers stretched wide open,
smelling of newly cut grass,
a luxurious outdoor world,
languorously gentling our days.

Looking Back from Fifty Years Forward

I remember Time standing still on the horizon
like a Colossus in his stone-etched stride.
We were young then, invincible,
joined at the hip with dreams of wonderful worlds.

Like Colossus in his stone-etched stride,
we loomed larger than life,
joined at the hip with dreams of wonderfilled worlds.
In the fifties, when Elvis was king,

we loomed larger than life.
Bright with raw hope, white dresses, white shirts,
in the fifties, when Elvis was king.
JFK had found Jackie; all was right with the world.

We graduated into dreams of kind futures.
We were young then, invincible.
The smiles on our faces tell of wonders to come.
I remember Time standing still along the horizon . . . .

That Last Time

I remember how
they used to run
from the front yard
to the back,
laughing when they beat
our car rounding
the u-shaped street,
waving good-bye
for a second time.

And as the car turned
down the avenue,
I always sneaked
another glance through
the car's side mirror.

Even after that last time together,
his arm circling her shoulder
in the quivering mirror
of time present, time past,
they are still waving—

to the eyes of my heart,
they are still waving.

An Omniscient View

Mother and progeny
I am to you,
due to a camera's lens
over a hundred years ago.

I look into unlined faces
and hearts holding dreams
yet to be born.

I want to answer
with a hind-sight given truth
the questions still unformed in those hearts.

A part of me, like a mother, wants to whisper:
"It will all work out, you know.
You'll meet the tests.
You'll survive.
That, too, can mean happiness."

He sits, holding his first-born.
No smile is allowed.
His wife stands stalwart
near his side, hand on chair,
a bit behind.

She stands there,
in long dark skirt and lace.
Only her eyes seem alive.
Like a startled sparrow,
she stares straight ahead,
not quite sure of her response.

New world.
New wife.
New mother.

Like a mother,
I look down the long road
she will travel.
The children she will bury
will change her.
Both will bury their dreams for the future
alongside the graves of their children.

From then on,
Life was only something
meant to be endured . . .

Happiness was not an option.

The Grandmothers

Why didn't they write their own herstory?
The old ones, the grandmothers?
Sometimes you find them fixed in photographs forever young,
before death claimed them in childbirth.
The rest you find staring with unsmiling faces
beyond the reach of the camera's eye—
hair pulled back tightly in round little buns,
wrinkled hands shielding tiny, squinting eyes.
They might have been dragged there
from the stove, apron-clad,
resentful of their time being wasted.
Ask posterity how much
it matters now whether the roast burned
or whether beds had been made that day
or whether or not dishes were still in the sink.
Their lives never ventured down roads to the future.
Only now would daughters of daughters
have loved hints full of finding happy alongside of clean.

No Room for Doubt

I can still remember
sitting low in the seat
of the darkened theater
with my best friend beside me

while mesmerizing colors
washed through the words
sung by Snow White
and splashed their way
right into us.

"Some day my prince will come,"
her pretty red mouth sang softly.
A second time followed right after—
louder, higher,

insistent.
No room for doubt.

And little birds twittered,
skittering right off the screen
in time
with the music.

And it all seemed so right.
The way it was supposed to be.
Life-true.
Heart-true.

We didn't know then
that Prince Charming
could walk out the door

leaving behind children
still needing to be raised
and listened to and loved
and paid for
through mortgages and heating bills
and trips to the orthodontist's

and food for bodies
that would insist upon growing
no matter what the weather

outside
or within.

And my best friend and me?

We left the theater
arm in arm
singing Snow White's song
at the top or our lungs,

especially that second line
that was so insistent,
leaving no room for doubt.

Under the Bed

We could play paper dolls
for hours on end,
my best friend and me.

First, pressing out the dolls
along the perforated lines
on colored cardboard.

Next, cutting out each outfit,
careful not to rip the white tabs
at the top for attaching to the dolls.

Finally, we would each choose,
ready at last to step
into those one dimensional worlds

there on the bedroom floor,
tryng on all those outfits,
trying on new lives.

It never occurred to us
that future pain
might flatten us out,

render us voiceless,
leave us in the dark
when finished with us—

fragile as the tissue paper
we wrapped the dolls in
when we were finished,

putting them out of sight
into the dark
under the bed.

Under Water

She really was such
a beautiful doll with
long straight yellow yarn hair
falling all the way down her legs—
Sparkle Plenty was her name.
I remember Angela from down the street,
the one who was older than me and who
always knew more than me and how she
kept hinting—"How much prettier she'll
be when we wash her hair!" How I loved
this doll just the way she was. How I
remember something deep down inside
me sobbing "no—no—no" when I went
ahead and dunked her under the water.
How Angela laughed when her hair
never did become untangled. How I think
of this whenever other angelas come into
my life. When that child in me thinks
others always know more than me, are
better than me. Whenever I send
my own sense of self underwater—
again.

Family Rituals

Our family rituals define us.

They take us
by the hand
and lead us

like little children

to the still fixed point
within the wandering heart
and say—

"Look.

Here
you
Are."

Trail's End*

"I will arise and go now, for always night and day
I hear lake water lapping with low sounds by the shore;
while I stand on the roadway or on the pavements grey,
I hear it in the deep heart's core."

"Lake Isle of Innisfree"—William B. Yeats

*Name for the family cabin located in northwestern Connecticut

Trail's End Reverie

"I made a deal
with the man upstairs,"
he would always say
with that slight twinkle
in his eyes.

So sure of this pact
and its promise.

He would find his way
back here,
drifting with the winds
through the tops
of these evergreens,
pausing to hear
the cawing of the chicken hawks,
drinking in the lingering rays
of the setting sun
before night would envelop all.

Sometimes
when I lean against
these warmed rocks
at the close of day
just the way he did,
and hear the silence
sing its song to me there,

I picture him, too,
once again pausing
to embrace this land
that always owned him—

and, now, owns me.

Cannavo Spring
Winsted, Ct.

The man who donated
this spring to posterity
probably was like you or me

in one of our better moments
when we think past
an immediate return.

He probably imagined
the high thirst of summer days,
the kind that only cupped hands
lifting water from a mountain spring
could possibly assuage.

He probably thought
of the horses, too,
bearing the burden of man,
day after day
with his journeying.

To a simple soul,
such a respite
along with a cool breeze
on an upturned face
was all that one should yearn for.

And this man
making his gift
a spring to the future

unknowingly

left the fingerprints
of his soul behind

for us to draw hope from,
along with the water.

Hop-scotch

The way light falls here
in late afternoon
gentles the day.

A resiliency pours itself out
through the tops of the oaks,
filtering its way down

through the hemlocks' darkness.
Forced to weave in and out
along the forest floor,

it reminds me
of my hopscotch days
from long ago.

Jumping around the stones
lying here, there, within the squares,
agility became a second nature.

So too, with this glorious light.
Accommodating its rays
to the density infiltrating

its way forward,
nothing else near offers
such fluidity, such grace.

And sometimes, after a quiet rain,
droplets of water mirror this light
all the way along the path

as far as the eye can travel.
A muted silent joy
sparkles valiantly through

to the other side
of the enveloping darkness.
Hopscotching all the way.

Trail's End
Winsted, Ct.

Either Way

There is
something to be said
about belonging to a place.

In my childhood
I would sit upon the rocks
outside this cabin window,
my doll in her shoebox bed,
acorns my imaginary dishes,
and play the day away.

The warm breezes
slipping through the tall hemlocks
would cool me
like they do now.

Once in a while,
birdsong—solitary, clear.
The buzzing of a motorboat
on the lake below.
Rustling tree tops, swaying.
A screen door, slamming shut—

and silence.
The kind you drink deeply from
and are nourished by,
without even knowing.

This mountain landscape
sitting at the end
of a climbing, curved trail
with sunlight dancing its way
through dark-trunked trees,

so much taller now
than in my youth,
creates long shadows
where none used to be.

Otherwise,
there is a sameness
to the days.

Then
sitting on the rocks,
content in my outdoor world,

Now sitting
above them,
listening to an inner one.

Lost
in a landscape
either way.

Floating

Over my head I watch clouds
skittering across a blue sky,
like little boats on water.
Up on the road past the sand,
tires on asphalt return sound
to the quiet.
The setting sun spills light
along the wanderings of the water.

To my right,
the large oak tree with its branches extended
over the beach in welcome
begins to darken
from the gradual withdrawal of the light.
A slight breeze
ripples through from somewhere,
perhaps from my youth, remembering

same lake.
same tree.
same sun.
same me?

My Wilderness

As a child I'd known these woods
rife with pink laurel in June,
where I remember one night
a majestic owl sitting
on a high branch of the oak
in front of the cabin,
thrilling and scaring me
all at the same time.
I loved that world with its
little woods weaving on and on,
carefully holding the darkness

snarled in the hemlocks' branches,
while allowing the stars,
so high and bright above
the tops of the highest oaks,
to stream pathways of light
along its pine-needled floor,
that allowed morning's orange
to break through as a grand surprise
most days of high summer.

But it is the heart-searing
call of the chicken hawks
that has never left me,
that first hinted to me
of life's essential loneliness,
that first linked my soul
to the solidity of this place

never to release its hold,
even now, while I grow old.

Dynamite, Pop, and an Indian named Charlie

Today, and turning
the faucet in the cabin. No water.
Click-click-click. Nothing.
Fuses. Wires. Pump. Well.
Where to begin?

Memory
Trips backward to being 10
and the sound of the dynamite
blasting through ledge, such shaking,
and then the sound of the water.
My Pop's friend, Charlie, part Cherokee,
had led him to this place with his
dowsing stick. I touched the blue
veins bulging in his thin wrist,
trying to hold the stick upright.
I held on, too. How hard it was.
I was sure his veins would burst.

No sign
of water here among
the rocks under the trees.
Then. Now.

But Charlie had said, "Water."
His stick pointed down.
And Pop trusted him.

It took 3 loud blasts
and everything shook and the water
flowed cold, so cold into Pop's hand.

Finding the buried pipe now
where the water still flows
will translate into dollars,
not dynamite.

When I was 10
magic visited these woods
with an Indian named Charlie
and nestled down to stay.

Dollars can't compete
with the memory
of that magic.

Sometimes,
"We love the things we love
for what they are."
Hyla Brook—Robert Frost

Seasons

"Four seasons fill the measure of the year;
    There are four seasons in the mind of man . . ."

The Human Seasons—John Keats

Spring Song

A twisted crab-apple tree
with brittle limbs
and lightning-scarred trunk
still stands guard
at the edge of my grandfather's land
like a left-over Irish soldier
enclosed
in a stone-strewn field
held fast
against the passing of time.

More
than a century
has passed
since he planted its seed
and left

promising to return.

And each year,
when the winds wend their way warmly
in from the Atlantic,
and the days, one by one, become longer and livelier,
and the ground starts to swell under green grasses,
and the new morning light taps lightly on limb—

there is a remembering.

One side of the tree
bursts wildly into bud, then blossom.

And when the blossoms
are loosened by the breezes
and a sudden snow
scatters the pink sweet petals
all over the golden-green countryside

one hears with the humming of the heart
the slow sure strains of an ascending hope
rising through its emptied branches.

Question Asked by Grand-Daughter

"Gramma, did you ever get caught by forsythia?"

Yes!
Today forsythia caught me.
Its bursting, bright Yellow
seized me,
unaware.

Its Wildness called to me
in those bending branches
escaping confinement,
curling toward something, anything
away from its bulky center.

Today,
no landscaper's shears,
no conformity
to standards and substances.

Tomorrow
might be different.

Tomorrow
all might be contained again.

But Today?
Ah! Today . . .

The wild, rollicking Yellows
have caught me, unaware.

Sometimes

Sometimes there's an invisibility
to khaki-colored farmlands left fallow
throughout the growing season.
Wide expanses of no growing thing.
Scattered pieces of abandoned machinery.
A tread-bare tire swinging back, forth
from the limb of a lone tree.

Sometimes it takes a certain kind of faith
to see past the land's emptiness,
to see in the waiting
the farm land's awakening,
to hold oneself open,
like the land,
for a new growing season.

Taking Time

Walking one side of the street,
morning sun beats down on asphalt.
Heat waves ripple, then rise.
No breeze breaks through
the sun's oppressive hold.

Crossing to the river's edge,
shade at once releases its rest.
Nature runs her course here,
undisturbed.

Yet it took time for

the arms of the maple to grow giant,
overshadowing both lawn and bank,
fanning the breezes
blowing in from over the water.

It took time for

the wide-leaf bushes
to grow up the river bank,
to reach shoulder-high
when arriving at level ground.

It took time for

the explosion of color to weave
its way along the river's edge,
fostering the flowers growing wild
to yield their scents as one,
perfuming the breezes like incense.

Beauty and Balance abound
in such a landscape.

It took time, though.
It took time . . . .

Autumn's Moment

Leaves
take their
time falling
all the way down
to the waiting ground.
In no hurry, they coast
on the playful air currents
like surfers skimming rising waves
lost in the moment flying freely
one with the primal force that sustains them.

The wind whipped currents of daily living
can leave us staggering out of breath
and longing for a simpler time
to wend our way thru with grace.
Look to Autumn's moment
and its falling gold—
arresting Life
with Death so
near—and
Trust.

Around and Around

Ferris wheel turning
Fall season furling
leaves landing low

around my feet,
while my heart beat
reaches my mind

where awareness grows.
Rising, stooping slows
my bones; they know.

The winds wind down, hold back.
Something there is, without lack,
underneath such diminishment.

Where does such thought reside?
Does it rise like a tide
from within me

or do I slowly rise
under its guise,
a life lesson learning?

Ferris wheel turning
autumn leaves swirling
around and around.

Winter Solstice

Dark green trees
etched sharply in silver light
cast their long shadows
across the glistening snow.

These strong silent presences
speak
as surely as
any ancient sage.

Pointing to the distant stars,
they still send their roots
under and down through the earth
for the nourishment that sustains them.

Their home is here.
At the darkest time of the year,
they speak of a light invisible,
of an energy so strong, so silent, so enduring.

the spaces between

3 a.m.: moonlight. The wind has stopped.
From far off, sparks of light flicker coldly
through a thick absence.

As when the call of the hawks
through an overcast sky
pierces the space, then gone.

Or when a rising red horizon
sings silence through bare-limbed trees
still etched in night's silver light.

A green mailbox
with a crown of snow
brings some comfort of presence.

3 oclock: strong moonlight
far flung stars
whispers with no words.

Stream Song

I listened today
to an energetic
little mountain stream

    burble its way
    this way and that

        over the rocks
        under the foot bridge
        along the rail trail

    then doubling back
    in wider and wider arcs

finally unconstrained
loving the liquid looseness
of it all

    like a roll of ribbon
    unraveling itself

        through this quiet wild place
        and all the while
            singing
          its
        own
        sweet
      song.

A Still Life: Vacant Lot

Broken bits of asphalt
mounded with dirt, small rocks, debris
rise at the edge of the town's green fields,

sharing space with rusted oil drums,
some standing upright, others rolled over
as if sleeping off a night before.

Bunches of white daisies
splashing yellow velvet centers
sprout through the dirt, rising upward.

Some lean on the rolled over drums,
as if they could redeem them.

Ode to My Soul

Spring always brings me
A resurgence
of hope
with her nourishing handiwork
so resplendent,
leaning grasses as soft
as silk.
I slide my soul
into dreams
as if they were
solid
ground
held
in place with
sunshine
and nurturing rain.

Quickfire summer
and my soul
a flame
made of yesterdays,
dimly lit memories
of grey storms
consumed
by this devouring essence.

two inner landscapes,
two wardrobe changes:
my soul
transforms itself through these seasons
and
now
a
third.
And just
as beautiful,
but bringing a sadness,
a finality to fruition
ineffable
like painful premonitions.

universes, universes
seeded
since their own
inception
with a luminescent
decay. Nevertheless,
I see
this impulsive splendor
leading me toward
a subtle slowing—
autumn—
and each day more stripped
hunger
and scraps of frozen desire.

Like strangers
in new lands
who wait for just one
foot print
in a frozen terrain
and follow wherever
it leads,
I wait out
all endings
clothed in winter's
aging
landscape,
knowing
a
phoenix will rise.

And the moral of my ode
is this:
souls have seasons
reasons
and what is hidden from view
waits
watches
witnesses
just as all landscapes do
spring summer
autumn winter.

Celebration

"When you set out on your journey to Ithaca,
pray that the road is long, full of adventure, full of knowledge."

Ithaca—Constantine P. Cavafy

Celebration

The Story of Celebration

-1-

Once upon a time
long, long ago

when Spirit was young
and trying to find its place,

Celebration announced itself
in the thump, thump, thump

of the drum
coming in contact

with the heart
of human hands,

translating its need
to laugh and to learn

to weep and to hope and remember
into sounds loud and soft

making their way

into life on the planet.

-2-

Spirit and Celebration
spilled forth from man

like twin rivers rushing
from silent underground sources

suddenly set free
to nourish and replenish
what had become
brittle and barren.

Celebration could coax Spirit
to forget the dark times

and recall the promises
of the growing seasons

when light and warmth in abundance
could make want go away, disappear.

Sacred was born into memory
when the earth spilled forth her promises,

gladdening the heart of humanity
long before the gods opened their mouths.

-3-
and money?
the want of it
the lure of it
the need of it
the curse of it

had nothing to do
with Celebration at all.

-4-
Of course,
that was long, long ago,

when light would linger longer
and Spirit, feeling joy,

could call out to others,
and remember . . . .

Words for the Journey

Take a walking stick.
Whatever road you find yourself on
will need to test you.

There may be mud.
There may be pot-holes.
There may be twists and turns
you cannot make without
the quiet courage your stick affords you,
the way it holds you bound fast to an unforeseen future.
It must be used,
must be tempered by times past
when hope was young,
fed with the dreams of futures unfolding.

Take an empty burlap bag
flung over one shoulder,
a notebook,
a pencil.

This is to feed the certainty
that the journey will provide
a sustenance;
cold streams for cupped hands
ripe berries for open mouths
And when this occurs,
jot it down against the day
when faith falls flat out
in front of you,
refusing to take one more step.

Leave your bag empty.
Be vigilant.
Demons are lured to such places.

Unbutton your jacket
to the light of the sun.
Let its rays warm you
one step at a time.
Always hum a heart song
to keep yourself alert
along the way.

There may be pathless woods.
There may be landscapes without sounds
save only the beating of your own heart.

There may be fears fluttering on the breezes
whispering, "Turn back, turn back."
Imagine your way forward.
Just the way
you did as a child
when life was young and unhurried and without end.

Sometimes You Just Gotta Live

Fat is the first of the culprits
hiding in every snack
including my cherished Snickers bar.
It's listed on the wrapper as fact!

Next in line is Sugar
so sweetly spending her day
filling ice cream and all those cakes.
Nothing gets in her way.

A quieter one is Salt.
He'll say he's doing what he ought.
But all doctors agree
we have to wake up and see
something better needs to be bought.

Convenience stores are the worst.
Their shelves always stocked with all three.
It's really hard when on the run.
Nutrition can be a mystery to me.

I voiced my woes to the friendly young woman
working the register one day,
And with serious eyes and wisdom-filled words,
every one there heard her say:
"No offense, mam, but maybe it's time
that something has to finally give.
Blindfold your eyes and plug up your ears.
Sometimes you just gotta live."

Through the Company of Women

I was raised in a company of women.
A gift from my family to me.
And nothing else has ever compared
or ever allowed me to see

a kaleidoscope of loving
through good days and some, quite sad.
Each one had her foods to bring comfort
at holidays—everyone glad.

So allow me to introduce the aunties
through a signature dish—one by one.
And a memory or two might be with them.
They and their food—so much fun!

Loretta was a gentle soul
with warm brown eyes, a quiet voice.
Whenever she baked, I licked the bowl.
Her chocolate peanut butter icing, my number one choice.

Agnes was known for Baked Alaska.
She was the rich one, can't you tell?
All of us kids were afraid of her.
She really knew how to yell.

Catherine was the cookie maker,
yet I never saw a cook book.
In the kitchen, a mover and a shaker,
a whirlwind, really—we shook!

Nellie was the funny one
and such a great cook, as well.
Her cole slaw with peanuts—requested all the time.
Even my grandkids think it's swell!

Then there was sweet Auntie Florence,
the best cook of the bunch, it's true
cuz whatever she made
the frig we would raid
for leftovers to eat going home.

My mom was the youngest of the sisters
and made the potato cakes every Christmas Eve.
Not deviating from the Tradition,
I've mastered them, I do believe!

A whiz with leftovers was Mary
from my Dad's side—and her secret pie.
She could take anything out of the frig,
throw into a pie crust in the blink of an eye!

Last, but not least, dear Kay-Kay
a great cook—Definitely NOT!
Whenever she went to make me toast,
it burnt—right on the spot!

But how I loved this blackened toast,
buried—by then,—in butter.
When home I went
to my mom I would boast,
Auntie Kay's toast—great like no other!

What a great company of women
Now you've met them—one by one.
This time of year they stop by
with a cake or a pie . . . .
I bake and bake til I'm done.

Then their cards go back in the file.
Grease stains and all, through all these years.
But the memories stay close a bit longer.
Long enough to chase away fears.

For through the company of these women
and all that they had to tell
through the foods that they made,
their laughter and love
A life lesson was learned: All shall be well.

Standin' on the Highway

Our Daisy died.
Her engine choked once, sighed, went silent.

Her lights flickered, faded,
like eye-lids heavy with sleep, and went still.

A card out, a call made, the wait starts.
Night air grows brisk; dusk gives way to dark.

He starts to hum a tune.
I fuss and pace and grow cold and tired.

He hums toward me, louder
adding words to the sounds floating near.

"Standin' on the highway
watchin' all the cars go by"

His life is that whole note
sustaining the melody, even in the wind.

Mine, those little flagged eighth notes
flitting up, down-swirling all around.

He stands still
unafraid of the dark.

I look twice
at every moving shadow.

How like the years
and the songs we've sung

sometimes out of tune
and sometimes way too loud

but all things considered
we're still standing

out here on the highway
and we're still singing our song.

The Scent of Lilac

The lingering scent of lilac
wafting from the alcove
of the grey-stoned church

stirs up lavender-laced memories
of the forever bushes outside the windows
of my childhood home.

Like these tiny buds
overnight,
into blossom,

in the space of a heart-breath,
something closed,
opens

to a place never left,
where the cracked cookie jar
still sits precariously

on the top
of the washing machine
in the kitchen,

where the strong box
hidden for safe-keeping
still rests under the clothes,

where the roll of thunder
meant racing to those open windows
before the rain blew in.

And I am there
where I never left,
among such things.

And in the shadows
I can sense the presences
that held and still hold me safe.

Fast forward a life.
No difference.
For this scent

with its truth
side-steps time.
All love lives now.

Like Wind

"Come, my friends,
   Tis not too late to seek a newer world . . . .
                        Ulysses—Alfred Lord Tennyson

Like Fireflies

As the years go by
I favor old and battered things,
weathered souls, tattered wings.

Dulled memories
rise up to fly
as the years pass by.

A pressed rose
from a first love sings
of weathered souls, tattered wings.

Like fireflies flitting our way
lighting the dark, beautiful things
but soon—weathered souls, tattered wings.

I favor things used up—
an empty cologne bottle, a cracked cup.
Beauty bled dry as the years go by,
we weathered souls, tattered wings.

Wordscapes

1
unobtrusively
tip-toes on by
in soft lavender shades
stretching out luxuriously
all the way from pink to
purple

little voids lighten
like after spring rain

the sun slices through
in patches here, there

slipping drops now, then
onto poised petals,
soft, heavy-scented.

2
Precariously
whispers and sighs
soulfully, tenuously
in hues of grey
like pigeons and storms
and dawns

walking a tightrope
suspended in day-space

arms spread wide
balancing the body on beam

or the pen in hand, poised
with demons afoot
alighting from suspended
thoughts
then retreating
only to advance once again.

Fearful energy waxes,
wanes
like a little child
wanting to let go
of a hand, yet not—

two steps forward, one
back.

3
Meandering
is mindful
of light-filtered openings
along long country paths
resilient to footfalls
twisting and turning their
way
forward, always forward
through a maze
of seldom-traveled
walkways

across and around
sometimes in the mind

where pictures
come and go

fleeting images
from a past or present

strung loosely together
in no particular order

no meaning
just meandering.

4
enveloping
hugs and cherishes
all that is
in any particular moment

like incoming tide
to shore-line

spray-spewing
air and sand
non-discriminately

encompassing and
enclosing
into a bubble-shaped world
a new creation

5
prevaricate and
procrastinate
stuttering, muttering
stall and defer

6
flamboyant and myriad
light up the night
like lightening

striking
again and again
through the blackness

7
finally, the *centipede*
with pairs and pairs
of thread-like legs

lumbers along lightly
treading the land

dancing, dancing . . . .

Rising Temperatures

The tanks appear first
with long beaks jerking left, right
seeking out prey.

Falling bombs light up the sky.
Rapid gunfire, like thunder,
grinds all sounds into one.

Children run from the streets,
sensing the temperature rise
like a pot of water feeling
the ascending boil first
near its bottom,
close to the flame.

Mothers flee with their children.

And here in America?

Mothers stand by
as body bags
bring their children home.

Where can these mothers go?
What can these mothers do?

While the Bill of Rights lies,
lies sleeping,
positioned proudly
under bullet-proof glass.

Eating Leftovers

The company hired by the sheriff's department pulls up in front of the large brick house, the one with the foreclosure sign standing up from the mailbox. Four men dressed in black with gold letters emblazoned on their back hop down and walk quickly up the sidewalk. Efficiency. They have one hour to remove in garbage bags whatever they find here.

> **a disheveled doll in a corner**
> **a little pink glove, a broken cookie**
> **someone's childhood**

How methodical they are! No speaking. One to a room. Four rooms at a time. They have to stay on schedule. This is only the beginning of a very long day. So many miles to cover. So many dumpsters to fill. No such thing as falling behind. That's not what they're paid for. And besides, no paid overtime.

> **snapshots scattered here, there**
> **unopened mortgage bills piled high**
> **on the kitchen table, like food.**

yesterday, today, tomorrow

In 2006, Israel and Hezbollah headlined
the newspapers with a 7 day offensive.
Boots on the ground then still echo through
the pages of today's history with Hamas
and the Palestinians moving to center stage.

> **unrelenting rockets
> sail back through night skies
> forever fires unfolding**

In Darfur, 7 year old children are
raped. The old and infirm are killed
where they stand. Sudan's president
states over and over again for the
press, "not possible, not possible,
all lies." So sweet revenge's desire.

> **all over the globe,
> macabre matches volley
> back, forth, back, forth**

In Oregon, a housewife and mom
hires a hitman to dispose of her
husband. Self-described as "Miss
Goody-Two-Shoes," she suggests
bludgeoning with a crowbar.

> **as it was
> in the beginning
> is now and ever shall be?**

> **world with or without end.**

Amen.

Davids and Goliath

Each generation
sings its own song

with hardly a care
who croons along.

Is the key too high
for older voices

that drop over time
and no one notices?

Is it too raucous,
sharp sounds galore,

guttural utterance,
shaking sound-gore?

Oblivious Youth
mild manners long gone

intent on just this—
singing its song.

It may seem selfish
to us old geezers

who were raised to be
such people pleasers

in a gentler time,
manners at meals,

please, thank-you's, doors
opened,
no striking of deals.

But the future unfolding
breathes ominously

like a dragon spouting
fire—so confidently.

Guns on every corner
breed Goliath round the globe

and, once again, youth,
like David from of old,

are called forth in numbers
against overwhelming odds

to pick up their slingshots
and go forward, like gods

to slay the dragon
that grows from our greed

holding the banner of hope
to sow with their seed.

So if manners are dropped
and gentle ways long gone
too,

no matter what we say
nor even what we do

perhaps it's a future
demanding a new

merging of values,
manners with a twist

of steel-like focus
to blend us along

'cause each generation
will sing its own song.

Downsized

Poor little Pluto.
Minding its own business
circling round 'n' round the sun
through those vast silences,
never deviating from the course,
never gaining or losing weight,
never questioning the plan,
never withholding its energy
from the intricate dance of the larger System,

when suddenly,
the men who study the data
and track the outcomes
and do the labeling
from a distance

and calculate
and formulate
and postulate

arrive at new conclusions.
Pluto is planet no more.
Down-sized.

Sometimes,
everything that is a strength
can turn out to be a weakness.

It all depends
on who is doing the watching
and when
and why.

Defining Moments

Defining moments
for an individual,
for a civilization,
are rare.

In an instant,
the horizon solidifies.
Boundaries slide invisibly
into place.

Before.
After.

For an older generation,
Pearl Harbor.
The unimaginable burst forth
on the consciousness of the world.

Hiroshima.
Nagasaki.

A veteran once said:
"Seeing someone Japanese
years afterward,
the hair would rise
on the back of my neck."

For another generation,
Kennedy.
A pink blood-stained suit
indissolubly bound
to staccato sounds
slicing through the smiles
in a sun-swept sky.

a riderless horse
a three year old's salute
Forever linked
Forever locked
in a nation's collective psyche.

Frame by frame,
picture by picture, the loss of innocence
in slow motion
for a country
and her people.

For all present generations,
twin towers.
Televisions across the nation
flashed suicide bombers
bringing down the towers
again and again.

In the beginning
who could guess at
the possible numbers
of lives incinerated
in such an inferno?
This—beyond any scope
of reference.

The evil that men do
had, somehow, "upped the ante."
Looming, hovering,
not quite ending this time.

And as the years pass,
we are left with burning questions:
What do we live by?

"An eye for an eye,
a tooth for a tooth?"

"If a man strike you on one cheek,
turn to him the other?"

The future is arriving each day
on the memory of that living nightmare.
But it is still full of promise
because it is the future,
praying a young dream of peace.

Are we growing any wiser?
Is our strength learning
to bend in changing winds
and dark places?

Only in time will we know.
For it is the passing of time
that will define us—

Before.
After.

Wishes and Stars*

words
spelled
in blood
tell
of man's
darkness.
thirty
thousand
babes
crawl
their
way
forward
into
uniform

picking up
rifles,
raising them
reluctantly
toward night
skies

taking aim
at
shimmering
star shine

just
like
blowing out
candles
on childhood
birthday cakes.

Make a Wish.

.

Weep
Wishes
Upon
Wishes.

Star-light
Star-bright
First star
I see tonight.

Wish I may
Wish I might
have this wish
I wish tonight.

Please
replace
the
stars.

Please help us
follow
their
lead.

Like
those
men
so long
ago
did

whom
all
called
wise.

* *During the Christmas season of 2009, the President
announced the addition of 30,000 troops for deployment to
Afghanistan.*

I trust . . . .

the sun's orange rising each daybreak
through tired b lack branches.

stars with their sharp, silent twinkling
when night's deep darkness appears.

the white fluff of clouds to appear
sooner or later in a blue-swept sky.

tides ebbing out
to always return.

But more.

I trust
love lacing its way
through all relationships,
weaving new meaning into each day.

I trust

the myriad, mysterious forms
it may announce itself through,
even the walls it can erect.

I believe that

over and through
under and around
beyond and behind,

love is always in process,
growing intensity, awareness
all around us, all around.

I trust . . .

the heart to keep on searching,
to keep its own fires kindled,
and, when left alone,
to always keep finding its way.

Wheels and Tines

A spindly horse rake
long given over to rust
sits abandoned at the edge

of this snow-stubbled field.
With no rider on its seat,

its darkened wheels and tines

starkly silhouette themselves
against the barren back
of approaching night . . .

So easy to imagine
the constant rhythms of horse, rider
with tines combing, separating.

Wheels turning, dawn to dusk,
down row upon row upon row
yielding a finished fabric at day's end.

But now
this field lies empty
long after the energy

of this place
has plowed its way forward
to a future

already forming
itself
into another quiet past.

Age speaks to me here.
Loss remembers so many fields.
Rust, for the moment shines gold.

The Wheel Turns*

The word
that is light
takes flight.
An eternal spark
flames, focuses.
Eyes see.
Hands touch.
Legs walk.
Ears hear.
A mouth opens.
Laughter erupts.
Spilled sound.

Simple childhood
rests
in easygoing joy.
Exhilaration
with being alive
commingles
laughter with tears.
A path
to a future
is lit
with beams
bright with hope.

With adolescence,
Complexity begins.
Darker colors
swirl through
childhood's landscape.
Self-doubt and sorrow
introduce themselves
like strangers do
when meeting.
The flaming fire
Of first love
drowns in its own tears.

Dreams crystallize.
Life becomes known
through the paths
that are chosen.
Roles run their course.
Sometimes apart.
Sometimes together.
Comfort is found
in the sameness
of the days.
No time to stop.
"Hurry up, please, it's
time . . . ."

The clothes
of life's roles
lie folded
or put away
or abandoned.
The mirror reflects
an older self
unadorned and content,
naked
and
unashamed
before the dawn.

These days rest
beneath mortality's shadow . .
Life's transience
walks its way through
this hallowed space.
Inspiration steps forward
lifting its voice
to sing wisdom's song
to all
who choose to listen.
The wheel turns . . .

*Mandala—a circular shape
present in various cultures,
religions, symbolizing life*

I wish to express my gratitude to the members of the following groups: The Upper Delaware Writers Collective, (N.Y.) Charlotte's Web, (N.J.) and the Hemlock Farms Writers' Group (PA). Revisions for many of these poems were based on their suggestions, lovingly given.

This book was edited by Jeremy Joyell, a childhood friend, and Kathleen Murnion, a forever friend.

Thank you both.

Acknowledgements
Acknowledgements are due to the editors of the following publications where some of these poems first appeared.

Common Ground Review—"Wheels and Tines"
                                        Honorable Mention
Poetree—"Spring Song"
Poets from the Center—"Wordscapes"
                                              Judges' Choice
                                    "Spring Song"
                                              Editor's Choice
River Reporter Literary Gazette
                                    "Sometimes"
                                    "My Wilderness"
                                    "the spaces between"
Stillwater Review
                                    "A Still Life: Vacant Lot"
The Light in Ordinary Things
                                    "Eating Leftovers"
Voices from Frost Place
                                    "Question Asked b y Grand-daughter"
Voices from Here
                                    "Victory Gardens"
                                    "Cannavo Spring"